HERBS
USING

WENDY HOBSON

Harlaxton Publishing Limited
2 Avenue Road
Grantham
Lincolnshire NG31 6TA United Kingdom
A Member of the Weldon International Group of Companies.

First published in 1993.

© 1993	Copyright Harlaxton Publishing Limited
© 1993	Copyright design Harlaxton Publishing Limited
Publisher:	Robin Burgess
Design & Coordination:	Rachel Rush
Cover Photography:	Chris Allen, Forum Advertising Limited
	Pine shelves kindly supplied by Rudkins of Grantham
Food Photography:	James Duncan
Stylist:	Madelaine Brehaut
Home Economist:	Joanna Farrow
Illustrator:	Valerie Littlewood
Editor:	Dulcie Andrews
Typesetting:	John Macauley, Seller's, Grantham UK
Colour separation:	GA Graphics, Stamford UK
Printing:	Imago, Singapore

British Library Cataloguing-in-Publication data.
A catalogue record for this book is available from the British Library.

Title:	Herbs Using
ISBN:	1-85837-108-2

 # CONTENTS

 # INTRODUCTION

Anyone who grows herbs will be aware of the beauty
and fragrance they impart to the herb garden, flower
border, patio or window-sill. They have a myriad of
uses in the home, not only in cooking but also in
drinks, crafts, cosmetics and gifts.

Making the best use of your herbs requires only a few basic skills. This book gives you all the essential information to
start you off. It will show you the various ways of preserving herbs and the best means of storing them to retain their
essential qualities.

Once you have prepared your herbs, you can start to experiment with new sauces and dishes in the kitchen, bath
products or skin creams and beautiful, decorative arrangements with dried herbs, fresh sprigs or seed heads. Use the
ideas in the book to guide you and let your imagination do the rest.

 ## COOK'S NOTES

Standard spoon and cup measurements are used in all recipes. All spoon and cup measurements are level.
1 tablespoon = 15 ml spoon
1 teaspoon   = 5 ml spoon
As the imperial/metric/US equivalents are not exact, follow only one system of measurement.
Ovens should be preheated to the specified temperature.
Fresh herbs are used unless otherwise stated. If they are unavailable, use half the quantity of dried herbs.
Use freshly ground black pepper unless white is indicated. Salt and pepper is added according to your individual taste.

OPPOSITE: Potted herbs arranged in the light of a kitchen window

 # HARVESTING

It is important to harvest your herbs at their peak so that you preserve the maximum of their essential fragrances and flavours. Whether you are going to use them fresh in a salad, or dry them for crafts or culinary use, they should be at their best.

USING FRESH HERBS

Fresh herbs have only a limited lifespan before they begin to lose their qualities, so if you have herbs in the garden only pick what you need when you need it. Use a sharp pair of scissors so that you do not damage the plant; most garden herbs will benefit from such regular trimming.

If you need to store fresh herbs, wash them gently, taking care not to bruise the leaves. Shake them dry, then place them in an unsealed polythene bag and keep at the bottom of the refrigerator; they will last about a week.

LEAVES & FLOWERS

When you are harvesting herbs for preserving, pick them at their most aromatic. Choose a dry day, as the herbs need to be as dry as possible when you pick them and be up early; harvest in the morning when the dew has dispersed, before the midday heat.

Leaves should be harvested just before the herb comes into flower. Snip off sprigs about 10 cm/4 inches long, using sharp scissors so that you leave a clean cut and do not damage the tender stems of the plant. Flower heads should generally be harvested when the flowers have just opened and are in perfect shape; lavender flowers, however, should be slightly immature.

Deal with small quantities at a time for the best results and collect only from plants that are healthy, well-established and free from disease or pests. Handle the herbs carefully as they bruise easily and bruising will affect their flavour and aroma. Never leave cut herbs lying around waiting to be prepared as they will rapidly deteriorate; deal with them as quickly as possible.

OPPOSITE: Harvesting and storing herbs

 ## ROOTS & SEEDS

Roots are usually lifted in autumn at the end of the growing season, when they are mature and richest in stored food. Lift the whole root with a fork, being careful not to puncture the skin. Shake off excess soil and carefully wash the roots. Cut off the top growth and fibrous rootlets then cut the root into sections or slices.

Seed heads are ready for harvesting when the seeds are ripe and brown, just before the plant is ready to shed them. Check the seed heads by rubbing one between your palms; the seeds should shed easily. Put a muslin (cheesecloth) or paper bag over the seed head and secure with a twist-tie or twist of wire. Now the seed heads can be snipped off without losing any of the seeds.

 # PRESERVING

The most common way to preserve herbs is to dry them and this method is perfect for many common herbs. There are other techniques, however, which are more appropriate to particular herbs and preserve their qualities more effectively.

DRYING IN TRAYS

Drying eliminates the water in the herb but retains its essential oils. Whichever drying method you use, herbs should be dried quickly at an even temperature, out of direct sunlight. The air must be able to circulate round the herbs and it is best to keep individual herbs separate as they are drying.

To dry herbs naturally, spread the herb sprigs, roots, petals or seed heads evenly over trays lined with sheets of absorbent paper, such as newspaper. For large-leafed plants, such as lovage and comfrey, remove the leaves from the sprigs before you dry them. Leave the herbs for a week or so until completely dry, turning them regularly and replacing the paper if it absorbs too much moisture. Roots will take a little longer.

If you dry herbs regularly, it is worth making a drying frame. Stretch muslin (cheesecloth) or fine netting over a rectangular wooden frame and lay the herbs on the frame to dry. The frames can be stacked on top of one another as long as there is about 5 cm/2 inches between them. Place new herbs on top of drier ones as the moisture will rise.

You can speed up the drying process by placing the trays or frames in a warm airing cupboard for three or four days. Alternatively, you can dry them in the plate-warming section of a cooker or at the bottom of a conventional oven with the door ajar, leaving the oven on its lowest setting for a few hours. If you have a traditional fuel-burning stove, you can dry the herbs in the slow oven.

The most modern method is to use the microwave. Spread out the herbs on three layers of paper towel and cover with another sheet of paper towel. The herbs will take only 2-3 minutes on high, but will be ruined if you leave them too long. Therefore, it is best to microwave for 30 seconds, check and turn them over, then continue in short bursts until they are dry.

Herb flowers, such as camomile, feverfew, lavender, sorrel or tansy, sprigs such as rosemary, sage or bay, or seed heads such as fennel, can be air-dried in bunches. Tie four or five herb sprigs loosely into a bunch by the stems and hang them upside-down in a dry, well-ventilated room where the temperature remains constant, keeping them out of direct sunlight. A spare room, dry attic or bedroom are all suitable.

When drying herbs with large flower heads, such as chives, the flowers must rest on a wire mesh screen with the stems hanging down, as the drying stems cannot stand the weight of the flower heads. Large seed heads, such as fennel, lovage, caraway or chervil, or large herbs such as angelica, can be dried upright in empty vases.

PREPARING & STORING DRIED HERBS

Once the herbs are dry, they will feel crisp and papery and will snap easily between finger and thumb. To remove the leaves from small-leafed herbs, run your fingers down the stalks and the leaves will rub off. For herbs with larger leaves, you may need to hand-pick the leaves from the stalks then crumble them between your fingers, or place the leaves in a paper bag and crush them with a rolling pin. Another method is to rub the herbs through a fine mesh before discarding the stems.

Dried herbs must be stored in airtight containers, preferably in a dark cupboard. The containers should be labelled with the name of the herb and the date of preserving. Even dried herbs will not keep indefinitely so do not dry in larger quantities than you are likely to use.

Seeds can simply be shaken off the dried flower heads then sieved or hand-picked to remove unwanted chaff. If you are storing them for planting the following season, wrap them in foil and then seal in an envelope labelled with the name of the seed, the date of collection and any other details such as the variety or flower colour. Seeds for culinary use can be stored in an airtight jar, labelled with the name of the seed and date of preserving and kept in a dark cupboard.

USING DESICCANTS

To preserve complete flower heads for dried arrangements or to garnish pot-pourri, desiccants are used; these are crystals that absorb moisture from a flower while preserving its shape. The easiest to use is silica gel which you can buy from the chemist or pharmacist. Grind it down in a food processor or with a pestle and mortar until it is as fine as caster (superfine) sugar.

Spread a layer of desiccant in the bottom of a plastic box. Arrange the flower heads on the surface and cover with desiccant gently, sprinkling it between the petals. Dry bell-shaped flowers upside-down so that the bells fill with desiccant. Seal the box and leave it undisturbed for five days, during which time the silica crystals will turn from blue to pink. Brush off a little of the desiccant and, if the flowers are dry and make a rustling, papery sound when moved, remove them from the box and brush them clean.

Bend a small hook at the end of a piece of florist's (floral) wire and push it through the flower head, pulling it back to secure it. Wind gutta-percha tape diagonally round the stem to cover the wire and store the delicate flowers upright in dry florist's foam (styrofoam).

Reactivate the desiccant by spreading it on a baking sheet and placing it at the bottom of a low oven until its colour turns back to blue. Sieve it to remove any particles and store for future use.

 **FREEZING**

Herbs that lose their flavour when dried can often be successfully frozen; chives, tarragon and parsley freeze well, as do mint, thyme, marjoram, borage, lemon balm and small flower heads such as chives. Wash and dry the herbs, then either strip the leaves off the stem or leave the sprigs intact. Place the herbs in a colander and pour over boiling water to blanch them; this kills the enzymes which cause the herbs to lose their flavour and colour. Shake them dry in a clean tea-towel (dish cloth) and place small quantities in freezer bags, suck out as much air as possible through a straw in the neck of the bag, seal, label and date. You can of course make up your own herb mixtures before you freeze them. Once frozen, the herbs will crumble in your fingers and will not need to be chopped for culinary use.

Tiny sprigs of herbs, chopped herbs or herb mixtures can be placed in ice cube trays, covered with water and frozen. Once frozen, tip the cubes into freezer bags so that they are ready to add directly to soups, casseroles or drinks. Edible herb flowers, such as borage, can be frozen whole in ice cubes and used as an unusual garnish for summer drinks.

Rub larger-leafed herbs, such as basil, lightly on both sides with olive or sunflower oil and freeze between sheets of greaseproof (wax) paper.

ABOVE: Drying in bunches

NEXT PAGE: Preparing herbs for pressing

 11

Any herbs with thin leaves or petals are suitable for pressing. The pressed specimens can then be used in herbal crafts. Avoid herbs with thick, fleshy leaves and flowers and always select perfect sprigs, delicate flowers or individual leaves and petals. Snip them neatly, removing petals gently from thick flowers or cutting leaves or leaflets into small groups.

You can use a book or sheets of stiff card to press your herbs. A special flower press made up of a number of sheets of stiff card fixed together at the corners with butterfly screws is useful but not essential, unless you plan to do a great deal of pressed flower work. Protect books from flower dyes with sheets of white tissue paper. You will also need some blotting paper or absorbent paper the same size as the press or books and some heavy books or other weights if you do not have a press.

Lay the leaves and flowers on a sheet of absorbent paper, using plastic tweezers or a soft paint brush to lift or move them and making sure they do not touch each other. Cover carefully with another sheet and place them in the press, between the sheets of card or between the pages of the book. Tighten the screws, press the card down with weights or close the book and weight it down. Leave undisturbed in a warm room for about two weeks then check and change the absorbent paper; you may need to do this two or three times if the material is very moist. Leave for about six months; the longer the specimens are left, the less likely they are to fade when exposed to light.

PRESERVING IN OIL, VINEGAR OR SALT

By storing herbs in oil, you not only preserve the herbs but also create wonderful fragrant oils for use in cooking or cosmetics (p.50). You can also preserve herbs in vinegar, creating aromatic herbal vinegars for use in sauces, salad dressing, pickles and chutneys (p.16).

Large-leafed herbs, such as sage, can be stored layered in a jar with coarse salt. They will keep for several months and impart their own flavour to the salt.

PRESERVING WITH GLYCERINE

Preserving plant stems in a glycerine solution is suitable for some herbs, such as bay and sorrel. The technique darkens the leaves and makes them soft and pliable with a lovely sheen.

Pick perfect twigs in summer when the new shoots are growing. Whisk one part glycerine with two parts very hot water until thoroughly blended and and then pour the solution into a vase. Stand the twigs in the solution, making sure they reach the base of the container and leave them undisturbed for about two weeks until the tips of the leaves are brown and glossy. When they are ready, you can paint them with varnish or spray with hair lacquer to help to preserve them. Strain the solution and use it again.

OPPOSITE: Storing herbs in jars and containers

 # OIL & VINEGAR

By storing herbs in oil, you can preserve the herbs and create a fragrant oil at the same time. Herbal vinegars are simple to make and an excellent way of using your garden herbs.

HERBAL OIL

Herbal oils can be used for both culinary and cosmetic purposes. Most aromatic herbs are suitable; basil, tarragon, thyme and rosemary are particularly popular choices.

Half-fill a sterilized bottle or jar with fresh herb leaves, then fill to the top with good quality olive or sunflower oil. Stir the herbs to release air bubbles, making sure that the herbs are completely covered in oil. Seal the bottle or jar and stand it on a sunny window-sill or over a radiator for two weeks, shaking daily. Strain the oil, using the herb sprigs for cooking if you wish. For a stronger flavour, add fresh herbs to the strained oil and store for a further two weeks, then strain again. Bottle the oil with a fresh herb sprig, cover, label and store in a cool, dark place.

You can make a delicious mixed herb oil with a few sprigs each of tarragon and thyme, plus a clove of garlic, a dried red chilli pepper and a few black peppercorns. Goats' cheese can be marinated in this oil and used in salads of crisp lettuce and sorrel leaves.

HERBAL VINEGAR

White or red wine vinegar or cider vinegar can be flavoured with herbs and used in salad dressings, cooked recipes or to make cosmetics. Basil, chervil, marjoram, mint, tarragon, sage or thyme are all suitable, as are dill sprigs or seeds. Purple sage will impart a lovely colour to the vinegar and so do chive flowers. You can use combinations of herbs: equal quantities of mint, chives, basil and borage are effective.

Place about 60 g/2 oz/1 cup of lightly bruised, fresh herbs in a sterilized jar. Bring 300 ml/ 1⁄2 pint/11⁄4 cups of wine or cider vinegar to the boil, pour over the herbs, seal and leave to stand on a sunny window-sill for two weeks, shaking occasionally. Strain the vinegar through muslin (cheesecloth) or paper coffee filters into another sterilized jar, add a fresh herb sprig, seal and store in a cool, dark place.

OPPOSITE: Ice cubes, oils and vinegars flavoured with herbs

 # HERB COOKING

There are lots of interesting recipes in this chapter,
plus many ideas to encourage you to experiment by
adding herbs to your favourite recipes.

With a little imagination, you can find all sorts of ways to use herbs in your cooking, supplementing home-grown herbs with fresh herbs from the supermarket if necessary.

Fragile herbs–parsley, chervil, tarragon, mint and basil–are best used coarsely chopped as their leaves bruise easily. They are frequently used raw or added at the end of cooking as their flavour is lessened by heat. More robust herbs–rosemary, bay, sage and marjoram–are generally used cooked and they also dry more successfully than fragile herbs. Herbs should be chopped with a sharp knife until the they are the texture you require, or they can be ground with a pestle and mortar or in a food processor to release their essential oils.

HERBS IN SOUPS & STARTERS

Many plain soups can be given extra flavour with the addition of a few fresh herbs: chives or lemon balm are excellent in a potato or leek soup, sprinkle borage in a tomato soup, or add coriander (cilantro) seed to give extra spice. Parsley is often used to garnish soups but will release more flavour if it is stirred in just before serving or sprinkled in the bottom of the soup bowls. Cream or fromage frais can be flavoured with chopped herbs before they are stirred into soup. Croûtons are more tasty when they are fried with chopped garlic and a few chopped herbs.

Light vegetable starters will benefit from herb sauces: lemon thyme or lemon balm can be added to a white sauce made with a mixture of milk and stock to create a light, lemony sauce to coat vegetables such as broccoli. Prawns can be served on cucumber slices with a minty or chervil-flavoured mayonnaise, or tossed in flour spiced with ground coriander seed and fried quickly. Fish pâtés benefit from the addition of a little dill or parsley.

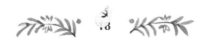

 **HERB COMBINATIONS**

A fresh *bouquet garni* takes only moments to prepare: simply tie together sprigs of thyme and parsley and a bay leaf. You can vary this traditional mixture by substituting sage or basil, rosemary, marjoram, tarragon or dill for either the parsley or thyme. Leave a length of string to tie on to the handle of the saucepan or casserole dish so that the *bouquet garni* can be easily removed before serving.

To make a *bouquet garni* with dried herbs, place spoonfuls of dried herbs in the centre of a circle of muslin (cheesecloth), gather up the edges and tie them into a sachet. A few sachets of *bouquet garni* in an attractive box makes a useful gift.

Fines herbes is made of equal quantities of finely chopped fresh herbs - tarragon, chives and chervil, sometimes with parsley - and added to savoury dishes at the end of cooking.

ABOVE: Muslin (cheesecloth) sachets of bouquet garni make attractive gifts

 ## Fried Sage Leaves

SERVES 4

24	fresh sage leaves
1 tablespoon	anchovy paste
60 g/2 oz/ 1⁄2 cup	plain (all-purpose) flour
90 ml/3 fl oz/5 tablespoons	water
	Salt and pepper
1	egg white, stiffly beaten
	A little oil for frying

Sandwich the sage leaves together with a thin spreading of anchovy paste. Beat the flour and water to a thick batter and season with salt and pepper. Fold in the stiffly beaten egg white. Dip the sage leaves in the batter and fry in hot oil for a few minutes until golden brown. Drain and serve hot.

Carrot & Coriander Dip

SERVES 4

225 g/8 oz/ 1 cup	chopped carrots
2	garlic cloves, crushed
200 ml/7 fl oz/ 3⁄4 cup	plain yoghurt
1⁄2 teaspoon	ground coriander seeds
	Salt and pepper
	Vegetable crudités

Cook the carrots in boiling water until tender then drain and rinse in cold water. Purée the carrots in a food processor with the garlic, yoghurt and coriander seeds until smooth. Season with salt and pepper. Spoon into a serving bowl and chill for 1 hour before serving with vegetable crudités.

OPPOSITE: CLOCKWISE: Sage and Cheese Scones (biscuits) (p.23); Carrot and Coriander Dip; and Fried Sage leaves

 # Parsley & Potato Soup

SERVES 4	2	rindless bacon rashers (slices), chopped
	30 g/1 oz/2 tablespoons	butter
	225 g/8 oz /1 cup	diced potato
	225 g/8 oz /1 cup	chopped onions
	450 ml/ ^{3}4 pint/2 cups	vegetable stock
	150 ml/ 1 4 pint/ 2 3 cup	milk
		Salt and pepper
	30 g/1 oz/ 1 2 cup	chopped parsley
	75 ml/2 1 2 fl oz/4 tablespoons	single (light) cream
		Garlic croûtons to serve

Dry-fry the bacon until the fat begins to run. Add the butter, potatoes and onions and fry until soft. Add the stock and milk, bring to the boil, cover and simmer for about 25 minutes until the vegetables are tender. Purée in a food processor then return to the pan, season with salt and pepper and stir in the parsley and cream. Reheat gently and serve garnished with garlic croûtons.

Creamy Sorrel Soup

SERVES 4	30 g/1 oz/2 tablespoons	butter
	1	onion, thinly sliced
	2	leeks, thinly sliced
	225 g/8 oz /6 cups	shredded sorrel leaves
		Pinch of freshly grated nutmeg
		Salt and pepper
	2	potatoes, sliced
	1.15 litres/2 pints/5 cups	vegetable stock, heated
	90 ml/3 fl oz/5 tablespoons	single (light) cream
	1 tablespoon	chopped chervil

Melt the butter and fry the onion for a few minutes until soft. Add the leeks and sorrel, stir well and season with nutmeg, salt and pepper. Cover and simmer gently for 5 minutes. Add the potatoes and simmer for a further 5 minutes, stirring occasionally. Add the stock, cover and simmer for 30 minutes or until the vegetables are tender. Purée in a food processor then return to the pan to reheat. Mix together the cream and chervil and swirl into the soup to serve.

HERBS, EGGS & CHEESE

Many herbs can transform the receptive flavours of
simple egg and cheese dishes.

Sprinkle a plain omelette with *fines herbes*, add chopped basil to a tomato omelette, or parsley to a potato omelette.
Snip some fresh chives into scrambled eggs for their delicate onion flavour. Coriander (cilantro), marjoram and savory
taste excellent with egg dishes and steamed, chopped sorrel makes wonderful light soufflés or flans.

Plain, fresh cheeses such as cottage cheese or cream cheese can be enlivened with almost any herb combination
and then used in sandwiches, on salads, with crackers, or as pancake fillings. Beat curd cheese with some eggs to
make a delicious flan (pie) filling. Stir some grated cheese into a basic white sauce and pour over lightly cooked
vegetables–sliced courgettes (zucchini), celery or celeriac, cauliflower or broccoli florets–or cooked pasta, sprinkle
with a mixture of breadcrumbs, grated cheese and a spoonful of chopped herbs, dot with butter and bake until golden.

SAGE & CHEESE SCONES (BISCUITS)

MAKES about 16	225 g/8 oz/2 cups	plain (all-purpose) flour
	1 tablespoon	baking powder
	30 g/1 oz/2 tablespoons	butter
	60 g/2 oz/^{1}2 cup	grated strong cheese
	1 teaspoon	French mustard
	2 tablespoons	chopped sage
		Pinch of cayenne pepper
	200 ml/7 fl oz/^{3}4 cup	milk

Mix together the flour and baking powder and then rub in the butter. Stir in the cheese, mustard, sage and cayenne
pepper, and gradually work in the milk to make a soft dough. Roll out on a lightly floured surface until 12 mm/^{1}2 inch
thick and cut into 5 cm/2 inch rounds. Reroll and cut out the trimmings. Place the scones (biscuits) on a greased
baking sheet and bake in the oven at 220°C/425°F/gas 6 for 10-15 minutes until golden.

 ## HERB CHEESE POTS

SERVES 4

175 g/6 oz/1½ cups	grated Cheddar cheese
3 tablespoons	double (heavy) cream
4 tablespoons	dry sherry
3 tablespoons	chopped winter savory or chervil
	A few bay leaves

Place all the ingredients except the bay leaves in the top of a double saucepan or in a bowl over a pan of simmering water and stir gently until melted. Pour into ramekin dishes, top with bay leaves, cover and chill until set. Serve with savoury crackers or wholemeal (wholewheat) bread.

SORREL & SPINACH TIMBALES

SERVES 4

1 tablespoon	butter
1	shallot, finely chopped
225 g/8 oz/5 cups	finely chopped sorrel leaves,
225 g/8 oz/5 cups	finely chopped spinach leaves
150 ml/ ¼ pint/ ⅔ cup	single (light) cream
2	eggs, beaten
60 g/2 oz/ ½ cup	grated Gruyère cheese
30 g/1 oz/ ½ cup	fresh breadcrumbs
	Salt and pepper

Melt the butter and fry the shallot until soft. Add the sorrel and spinach, cover and cook over a low heat until soft, stirring occasionally. Remove from the heat and stir in the cream, eggs, cheese and breadcrumbs and season with salt and pepper. Spoon the mixture into ramekin dishes and cover with foil. Stand the dishes in a baking tin filled with water to come half-way up the sides of the dishes. Bake in the oven at 180°C/350°F/gas 4 for 1 hour until firm to the touch.

 # HERBS for FISH

The delicate flavours of fish need suitably delicate treatment and herbs such as dill, tarragon and chives are often used. Oily fish, such as mackerel, will stand a more robust flavouring. Salmon is delicious marinated in pesto sauce (p.43) and white wine overnight and then fried, with the sauce being added gradually until the fish is cooked.

BAKED BREAM WITH THYME

SERVES 4

2	small bream
	Salt and pepper
8	thyme sprigs
4 tablespoons	olive oil
3	shallots, sliced
1	garlic clove, crushed
1	red pepper (capsicum, bell pepper), sliced
1	yellow pepper (capsicum, bell pepper), sliced
450 g/1 lb	tomatoes, skinned, seeded and chopped
6	anchovy fillets, chopped
	Juice of 1 lemon
	Thyme sprigs to garnish

Trim, scale and gut the fish. Make several diagonal slashes on the sides of the fish, season with salt and pepper and press a sprig of thyme into each cut.

Heat half the oil in a shallow, flameproof casserole and fry the shallots until soft. Stir in the garlic, peppers (capsicums, bell peppers), tomatoes and anchovies and fry until soft. Place the fish on top of the vegetables, sprinkle with the lemon juice and remaining oil and bake in the oven at 180°C/350°F/gas 4 for 30 minutes until the fish flakes when tested with a fork.

Transfer the fish to a warm serving platter. Cook the vegetables over medium heat until all the liquid has evaporated. Spoon around the fish and serve garnished with fresh thyme.

 **GRAVAD LAX**

Use as much or as little dill as you like for this classic Swedish dish.

SERVES 4	450 g/1 lb	salmon fillets
	2 tablespoons	coarse salt
	1 tablespoon	pepper
	1 teaspoon	caster (superfine) sugar
		Large bunch of dill
	4 tablespoons	brandy (optional)
Sauce:	2 tablespoons	French mustard
	1 tablespoon	caster (superfine) sugar
	1	egg yolk
	2 tablespoons	dill or white wine vinegar
	125 ml/4 fl oz/ $\frac{1}{2}$ cup	sunflower oil
	2 tablespoons	chopped dill
		Salt and pepper

Clean the fish carefully. Mix the salt, pepper and sugar and rub into the fish. Arrange a layer of dill on the base of a shallow dish and lay half the salmon fillets on top, skin-side down. Add another layer of dill and place the remaining salmon on top, skin-side down and head to tail so the fish is flat. Scatter any remaining dill on top and pour over the brandy, if using. Place a heavy plate or board on top, cover and chill for 48 hours, turning the salmon occasionally and basting with the juices.

To make the sauce, whisk the mustard, sugar, egg yolk and vinegar until thoroughly blended. Gradually add the oil a drop at a time, whisking continuously, until the sauce thickens. Stir in the dill and season with salt and pepper.

Discard the dill from the fish and brush off the salt. Cut in wafer-thin slices and serve with the sauce.

PAGES 26-27: Gravad Lax

 # MEAT & POULTRY

Almost any casserole will be enhanced by the addition of a few herbs, while grilled (broiled) meats can be garnished with fresh herbs or served with a herb sauce.

Use chopped herbs, or add herb sprigs for a stronger flavour, discarding the stems before serving. Thyme, bay or marjoram can be used with most meats. Rosemary and sage are best used with rich meats such as lamb or goose; but be careful with quantities as these herbs can be overpowering. The less pronounced flavour of chicken is enhanced by delicate herbs such as tarragon. You can add chopped herbs to dumplings, or rub meat with ground dill or caraway seeds before roasting.

Parsley and thyme or sage and onion are traditional combinations for stuffings made with fresh breadcrumbs, seasoned and bound with a beaten egg. Use the mixture to stuff large cuts of meat, for rolling into balls for frying, or to mix with minced (ground) beef and sausagemeat and bake as a meat loaf or wrap in puff pastry and serve sliced, hot or cold, with tomato sauce.

LAMB WITH ROSEMARY

Serves 4

1 tablespoon	olive oil
1 tablespoon	butter
2	garlic cloves, crushed
4	large lamb chops
1	rosemary sprig
300 ml/ 1⁄2 pint/1 1⁄4 cups	dry white wine
	Salt and pepper

Heat the oil and butter and stir in the garlic. Add the lamb chops and fry until browned on both sides. Add the rosemary and pour over the wine. Bring to the boil, partially cover and simmer for about 30 minutes until the lamb is just tender.

 # LIVER WITH CABBAGE

& CARAWAY

SERVES 4

1 tablespoon	butter
1 tablespoon	oil
450 g/1 lb	lambs' liver, cut into strips
1	onion, sliced
225 g/8 oz/2¹2 cups	shredded cabbage
1	crisp eating apple, peeled, cored and sliced
1 tablespoon	caraway seeds
2 tablespoons	herb vinegar
1 tablespoon	light brown sugar
	Salt and pepper

Heat the butter and oil in a large frying pan (skillet) and fry the liver until lightly browned then remove it from the pan. Add the onion and fry until soft, then add the cabbage and stir for 5 minutes until the cabbage begins to wilt. Stir in the apple, caraway seeds, herb vinegar and sugar and simmer over a moderate heat for 3 minutes, stirring. Return the liver to the pan and stir well for a few minutes until heated through. Season with salt and pepper and serve with rice and a green salad.

 # CHICKEN & TARRAGON

SERVES 4

1 tablespoon	oil
1 tablespoon	butter
4	chicken pieces
1	onion, sliced
1	carrot, sliced
250 ml/8 fl oz/1 cup	dry white wine
125 ml/4 fl oz/ 1⁄2 cup	chicken stock
3 tablespoons	single (light) cream
1 tablespoon	chopped tarragon
1 tablespoon	chopped chervil
	Salt and pepper

Heat the oil and butter and fry the chicken until browned on all sides then remove it from the pan. Add the onion and carrot to the pan and fry until softened. Return the chicken to the pan, cover and cook over a low heat for about 20 minutes until it is cooked through. Transfer the chicken to a warm serving plate and keep it warm. Skim off any fat in the pan, pour in the wine and stock and bring to the boil, stirring to scrape up the meat juices. Boil for 3 minutes then stir in the cream and herbs and season with salt and pepper. Heat the sauce through gently before pouring over the chicken to serve.

NEXT PAGE: CLOCKWISE: Carrot Salad with Fennel (p.35); Chicken and Tarragon; Mangetout (Snow Pea) Salad with Basil (p.35)

 **SALADS & VEGETABLES**

A few whole herb leaves such as chervil, basil, tarragon, parsley, mint, sorrel, or comfrey, give a new flavour to a green salad or you can create an unusual and colourful salad with a few crisp lettuce leaves and tomato and cucumber slices with some apple mint, sorrel, sweet cicely and marigold leaves, nasturtium flowers and violets, tossed in a herb vinaigrette dressing. Be adventurous with your combinations.

Use different vegetables in salads, not just salad leaves. Potato salad can be dressed with chive-flavoured mayonnaise; sliced beetroot is delicious topped with soured cream mixed with chopped dill. Use herb oils or vinegars for salad dressings or mayonnaise as an instant way of adding flavour and interest. Courgettes (zucchini) taste wonderful sliced in julienne strips and marinated in herb mayonnaise for several hours.

Vegetables, too, cry out for herb dressings, sauces, or a few herbs in the cooking water to enhance the flavours. Potatoes go well with mint, chives, caraway and dill; mushrooms and tarragon make an interesting combination; fennel gives a mildly aniseed flavour to celery or leeks; thyme goes well with aubergines (eggplants), courgettes (zucchini) or carrots; parsley enhances the flavour of parsnips.

Use herb butters (p.44) to garnish steamed or boiled vegetables, mixing in a little lemon juice for a sharper taste. For an appetizing courgette (zucchini) dish, soften a sliced onion in olive oil, then fry some sliced courgettes (zucchini) with a generous sprinkling of snipped chives until tender and golden.

Potatoes baked in their jackets can be made into a delicious light meal. Scoop out the potato flesh and mash it with a knob of butter, a beaten egg, some snipped chives, chopped mint or parsley and grated strong cheese. Pile the mixture back into the potato shells and flash under a hot grill (broiler) until golden.

 ## CARROT SALAD

WITH FENNEL

SERVES 4

2 tablespoons	chopped fennel leaves
350 g/12 oz/3 cups	grated carrots
2 tablespoons	olive oil
1 tablespoon	lemon juice
1 teaspoon	Dijon mustard

Mix together the fennel and carrots. Whisk the olive oil, lemon juice and mustard together, pour over the carrots and toss well. Cover and chill for at least an hour before serving, stirring occasionally.

MANGETOUT (SNOW PEA) SALAD WITH BASIL

SERVES 4

175 g/6 oz/2 cups	mangetout (snow peas)
	Salt
2	courgettes (zucchini), sliced
2	shallots, sliced
3 tablespoons	chopped basil
4 tablespoons	olive oil
1 tablespoon	orange juice
1 tablespoon	red wine vinegar
1 teaspoon	clear honey
1	garlic clove, crushed
	A few orange slices to garnish

Blanch the mangetout (snow peas) in boiling, salted water for 2 minutes then drain and pat dry on paper towels. Mix with the courgettes (zucchini), shallots and basil in a salad bowl. Place the oil, orange juice, vinegar, honey and garlic in a screw-topped jar and shake until blended. Pour over the salad and toss well. Cover and chill for a few hours before serving, garnished with orange slices.

 # ROSEMARY TURNIPS

SERVES 4

450 g/1 lb	small turnips, sliced
1 tablespoon	butter
1 tablespoon	sunflower oil
2	garlic cloves, crushed
2 tablespoons	chopped rosemary

Cook the turnips in boiling water for about 5 minutes until they begin to soften. Drain well. Melt the butter and oil and fry the turnips, garlic and rosemary until golden.

BAKED TOMATOES WITH BASIL

SERVES 4

450 g/1 lb	tomatoes, sliced
1 tablespoon	caster (superfine) sugar
	A handful of basil leaves, coarsely chopped
	Salt and pepper
300 ml/ 1⁄2 pint/1 1⁄4 cups	double (heavy) cream
60 g/2 oz/1 cup	fresh breadcrumbs
30 g/1 oz/2 tablespoons	butter

Layer the tomatoes in a shallow ovenproof dish, sprinkling each layer with sugar, basil, salt and pepper. Pour over the cream, sprinkle with the breadcrumbs and dot with the butter. Bake in the oven at 180°C/350°F/gas 4 for 30 minutes until golden brown.

OPPOSITE: Baked Tomatoes with Basil; Liver with Cabbage and Caraway (p.30)

 ## DESSERTS & CAKES

Spices are more often associated with desserts but
herbs should not be forgotten.

Basil can be sprinkled over baked apples, rosemary imparts a lovely fragrance to ice-creams, while lemon balm, marjoram and caraway can be added to fancy breads.

Vanilla pods (beans) are not the only ingredients that can be used to flavour sugar for making ice-cream, cakes and puddings. Add a few sprigs of mint, bay, rosemary or thyme, or a few lavender flowers or rose petals to a jar of caster (superfine) sugar and leave for a few weeks, stirring occasionally. Use a tablespoon or two of the sugar mixed with ordinary sugar for baking and keep the jar topped up. Replace the herb after a few months.

Scent clear honey with fragrant herbs such as rosemary or lavender to give a delicious new flavour in baking, to decorate ice-cream or plain yoghurt, or to spread on hot toast. Divide 450 g/1 lb/1$\frac{1}{2}$ cups of honey between two jars and stir in 250 ml/8 fl oz/1 cup of washed and dried leaves or petals. Cover the jars, stand them on a folded cloth in a saucepan and fill with water to come three-quarters of the way up the jars. Bring to the boil, then simmer for 30 minutes. Leave to stand for 24 hours. Strain the honey into sterilized, warm jars and discard the herbs.

Crystallize (candy) fresh herb flowers or mint or lemon balm leaves to decorate desserts. Wash and dry the flowers, brush them on all sides with whisked egg white and sprinkle them with caster (superfine) sugar. Stand them on a wire tray in an oven on the lowest setting with the door ajar until dry.

Try replacing the oil in bread or cake recipes with herbal oil, or use a herb tea to make tea ice-creams or tea bread. Add chopped herbs to any standard bread recipes; sage and chopped shallots are delicious in granary bread.

ROSEMARY CITRUS SORBET

SERVES 4

225 g/8 oz/1 cup   *caster (superfine) sugar*
1.15 litres/2 pints/5 cups   *water*
   Grated rind and juice of 2 lemons
30 g/1 oz/ ^{1}2 cup   *rosemary sprigs*

Dissolve the sugar in the water over a low heat then boil for 3 minutes; divide the resulting syrup in half. Add the lemon rind to one half and simmer gently for about 8 minutes. Add the lemon juice and leave to cool. Add the rosemary to the other half, bring to the boil then remove from the heat and leave to infuse for 15 minutes. Strain the rosemary syrup into the lemon syrup, leave to cool and then chill. Pour into a freezer tray and freeze for 2 hours. Turn into a bowl and beat well then return to the freezer tray until firm. Serve garnished with rosemary sprigs.

ABOVE: Herbs being used to flavour sugar and honey for desserts.

NEXT PAGE: Lemon Balm Ice-cream (p.42); Herb Soda Bread (p.42)

 # HERB SODA BREAD

You can use a variety of herbs for this simple soda
bread, or substitute 1 tablespoon of chopped dill,
caraway or fennel seeds.

MAKES 1 x 20 cm/8 inch loaf	*225 g/8 oz/2 cups*	*plain (all-purpose) flour*
	225 g/8 oz/2 cups	*wholemeal (wholewheat) flour*
	2 teaspoons	*salt*
	1 teaspoon	*bicarbonate of soda (baking soda)*
	30 g/1 oz/2 tablespoons	*butter*
	1 tablespoon	*snipped chives*
	1 tablespoon	*chopped chervil or parsley*
	300 ml/ 1⁄2 pint/1 1⁄4 cups	*milk*
	1 tablespoon	*lemon juice*

Mix together the flours, salt and bicarbonate of soda and rub in the butter until the mixture resembles breadcrumbs.
Stir in the herbs and mix to a soft dough with the milk and lemon juice. Knead into a round shape, cut a cross on the
top and stand the loaf on a greased baking sheet. Bake in the oven at 200°C/400°F/gas 6 for 45 minutes until risen
and firm. The loaf should sound hollow when tapped underneath.

LEMON BALM ICE-CREAM

SERVES 4	*300 ml/ 1⁄2 pint/1 1⁄4 cups*	*milk*
	10	*lemon balm leaves, crushed*
	3	*egg yolks*
	125 g/4 oz/ 2⁄3 cup	*icing (confectioners') sugar*
	300 ml/ 1⁄2 pint/1 1⁄4 cups	*double (heavy) cream*
		Lemon balm leaves to decorate

Bring the milk and lemon balm leaves to the boil then remove from the heat and leave to infuse for 40 minutes. Whisk
the egg yolks and sugar until pale and frothy. Strain the flavoured milk into the egg and sugar mixture and stir over a
low heat for about 15 minutes until the mixture thickens enough to coat the back of a spoon. Pour into a shallow freezer
tray, leave to cool, then cover and freeze until the ice-cream begins to set.

   Whip the cream until stiff and fold into the mixture. Freeze for a further 2 hours, beat again, then freeze until firm.
Place in the refrigerator to 'ripen' for 30 minutes before serving, decorated with fresh lemon balm leaves.

 # SAUCES, BUTTERS & JELLIES

Herbs form the basis of many raw sauces as well as flavouring cooked sauces. Almost any chopped herbs can be added to a basic white sauce, while a handful of blanched and chopped parsley, tarragon and watercress will completely transform an ordinary mayonnaise to serve with salads, fish, chicken or vegetables.

PESTO SAUCE

This is a classic Genoise sauce used for pasta and flavouring. It freezes well.

MAKES about 300 ml/ 1⁄2 pint/11⁄4 cups

60 g/2 oz/ 2⁄3 cup	basil leaves
6	garlic cloves
60 g/2 oz/ 1⁄2 cup	pine nuts
125 g/4 oz/1 cup	grated Parmesan cheese
175 ml/6 fl oz/ 3⁄4 cup	olive oil
	Salt and pepper

Purée the basil, garlic, pine nuts, Parmesan cheese and a little of the oil in a food processor or use a pestle and mortar. Add the remaining oil gradually, processing or pounding until the sauce emulsifies. Season with salt and pepper.

 **HERB BUTTERS**

Make herb butters with chervil, lovage, parsley,
mint, coriander (cilantro), basil, tarragon, or blend
together a selection of herbs. A little parsley and
lemon juice makes garlic butter less pungent.

Chop 3 tablespoons of fresh herbs and blend them with 225 g/8 oz/1 cup of unsalted butter. Roll into a cylinder on
greaseproof (wax) paper, twist the ends and chill, or wrap in foil and freeze. Serve sliced on grilled (broiled) meats or
fish, or use to top new potatoes or fresh vegetables, or to spread on crusty wholemeal (wholewheat) bread.

TOMATO & THYME SAUCE

You can vary this basic tomato sauce by adding
your favourite herbs.

MAKES about 450 ml/ ¾ pint/2 cups

30 g/1 oz/2 tablespoons	butter
1 tablespoon	olive oil
2	shallots, chopped
3	garlic cloves, crushed
450 g/1 lb	tomatoes, skinned, seeded and chopped
2 tablespoons	tomato paste
2 tablespoons	chopped thyme
	Salt and pepper

Heat the butter and oil and fry the shallots until soft. Add the garlic, tomatoes and tomato paste. Cover and simmer for
20 minutes, stirring occasionally. Add the thyme, season with salt and pepper and simmer for a further 5 minutes.

OPPOSITE: A medley of sauces. Herb butter; Pesto sauce (p.43); Tomato and Thyme sauce.

 **MINT JELLY**

This traditional mint jelly makes a refreshing
change from mint sauce to serve with roast lamb or
other grilled (broiled) meats. You can also make a
similar jelly with parsley, thyme or tarragon.

MAKES about 2 kg/4½ lb	*2.5 kg/5 lb*	*cooking apples*
	1 litre/1¾ pints/4¼ cups	*water*
	4	*mint sprigs*
	1 litre/1¾ pints/4¼ cups	*distilled white vinegar*
		Granulated or preserving sugar (see method)
	60 g/2 oz/1½ cups	*chopped mint*

Wash the apples and cut them into chunks, without peeling or coring them. Place them in a saucepan with the water and mint, bring to the boil, cover and simmer for about 35 minutes until soft and pulpy, stirring occasionally. Add the vinegar and boil for 5 minutes. Pour the mixture into a jelly bag and leave to drain overnight without pressing or the jelly will be cloudy.

Measure the juice and add 450 g/1 lb/2 cups sugar for each 600 ml/1 pint/2½ cups juice. Stir over a low heat until the sugar has dissolved, then boil vigorously for about 8 minutes until setting point is reached. Test for setting by cooling a spoonful of the jelly on a chilled saucer; the jelly should wrinkle when pressed. Skim, if necessary, then stir in the chopped mint, pour into sterilized jars and label.

 # HERBAL DRINKS

Herbal tisanes have long been drunk both for pleasure and for their medicinal properties. Rather than buying expensive herbal teas from health food shops, make your own herb teas, refreshing iced herbal drinks, or traditional wine cups.

Wine Cups

Borage or chive flowers, or sprigs of fresh herbs such as mint—whether fresh or frozen into ice cubes (p.11) —make attractive garnishes for wine cups. Experiment with ingredients when you make your own wine cups. Start with a bottle of dry white wine, and add a few tablespoons of brandy and 60 g/2 oz/ $1\frac{1}{4}$ cup of herb sugar (p.38). Float a thinly sliced orange, apple and lemon in the wine and chill for 1 hour. When you are ready to serve the cup, add a bottle of sparkling rosé wine 1 litre/$1\frac{3}{4}$ pints/$4\frac{1}{4}$ cups of lemonade (soda) and stir well. Float some fresh apple mint sprigs and borage flowers in the wine just before serving.

You can flavour your own liqueurs to make original drinks or unusual gifts. Crush or purée 3 tablespoons of peppermint or lemon thyme leaves and add them to 600 ml/1 pint/$2\frac{1}{2}$ cups of wine or brandy with a few strips of orange rind. Make a honey syrup by boiling 75 ml/5 tablespoons of water with an equal quantity of clear honey until well blended. Add this to the liqueur, cover and leave to stand for three weeks. Strain the liqueur, bottle, seal and label.

 # HERBAL TEAS

Herbal 'infusions' are made by steeping fresh or dried herbs in boiling water; 'decoctions' are made by boiling the herbs for a few minutes before steeping. What we now call herbal teas are becoming increasingly popular and can easily be made with the leaves of sage, marjoram, borage, summer savory, thyme, rosemary, mint or lemon balm, or with camomile or elder flowers.

To make herbal tea, steep 2 tablespoons of the fresh herb of your choice in 250 ml/8 fl oz/1 cup of boiling water for a few minutes then strain. You can flavour the tea with clear honey or flower honey and float a slice of orange or lemon in the cup. Herbal seed teas made from fennel, caraway or dill seeds need only 1 tablespoon of the crushed seeds but should be left to infuse for 5-10 minutes.

ICED TEAS

Many herb teas, such as thyme and mint, taste excellent when flavoured with clear honey and chilled. Traditional tea can also be flavoured with herbs to make an aromatic and refreshing drink. Pour 600 ml/1 pint/2$\frac{1}{2}$ cups of strong hot tea into a jug and add two bruised sprigs of mint and the juice of half a lime. Leave to infuse for 30 minutes, then strain and chill. Sweeten with clear honey and serve with ice, mint sprigs and lime slices.

For a fragrant marjoram drink, dissolve 2 tablespoons of sugar in 250 ml/8 fl oz/1 cup of water then boil for 5 minutes to a syrup. Leave it to cool then chill. Process a handful of marjoram leaves with 4 tablespoons of water and the juice of a lemon. Stir into the syrup, cover and chill for at least 1 hour. Stir in 450 ml/ $\frac{3}{4}$ pint/2 cups of chilled, fizzy, mineral water and serve with borage-flower ice cubes (p.11).

OPPOSITE: A selection of herbal teas and drinks

 # COSMETICS

Originally toiletries and cosmetics were, of course,
all made from local, natural ingredients.

Today, cosmetics abound in chemists, department stores and specialist beauty shops but it is very satisfying to create effective and natural cosmetics of your own. What is more, herbal preparations have many beneficial qualities in addition to their distinctive fragrances. Lavender and camomile are relaxing, comfrey regenerates ageing skin, sage gives relief from aching muscles, spearmint and thyme are refreshing, rosemary and angelica are stimulating, while lovage is supposed to make you more lovable!

HERBAL SOAPS

You can add the herbal fragrance of your choice to unperfumed castile soap by grating the soap and melting it in the top of a double saucepan over simmering water. Stir in a teaspoon of almond or vegetable oil and a teaspoon of honey and stir over the heat for 5 minutes. Stir in a few drops of essential herb oil and leave the soap to cool and harden.

Soap used to be made with tallow but you can substitute vegetable oils and make your own soap, following the recipe below. Take great care when using the caustic soda. Vary the herbs you use, add honey or oatmeal and use a variety of different-shaped moulds such as jelly moulds, yoghurt pots or baking dishes.

300 ml/ 1⁄2 pint/11⁄4 cups	water
4 tablespoons	caustic soda
3 tablespoons	sunflower oil
90 ml/3 fl oz/5 tablespoons	olive oil
2 teaspoons	herbal oil (p.16)
3 tablespoons	chopped marjoram

Place the water in a glass bowl, add the caustic soda and stir with a wooden spoon until it has dissolved; the soda will heat spontaneously. Set aside until lukewarm. Meanwhile, warm the oils to the same temperature. Pour the oil slowly into the soda, stirring continuously, then add the marjoram and beat until the mixture thickens and turns opaque. Pour into moulds, stand on a cooling rack and leave in a warm, dry place for 24 hours until set. Remove from the moulds, wrap in greaseproof (wax) paper and leave in cool a place for 2 to 3 weeks to harden.

 ## FRAGRANT OILS

Natural oils which encapsulate the fragrance of the
flower or herb form the essence of many cosmetics.

Concentrated herbal oils must be purchased from a herbalist or chemist as there is great skill in preparing such items.
However, the following instructions will enable you to create light floral oils with scented flower petals. Use a
measuring jug to weigh the petals.

300 ml/ 1⁄2 pint/11⁄4 cups	*almond oil*
2.25 litres/4 pints/21⁄2 quarts	*flower petals*
1 teaspoon	*liquid storax*
1 teaspoon	*tincture of benzoin*

Warm the oil in the top of a double saucepan over simmering water. Add 450 ml/ 3⁄4 pint/2 cups of petals, stir, cover
and leave over a low heat for 2 hours, checking regularly to ensure that the pan does not boil dry. Strain and reserve
the flowers. Add another 450 ml/ 3⁄4 pint/2 cups of flowers to the oil and repeat the process until all the flowers have
been used.

Pour the oil and all the flowers into a large pan, bring to the boil slowly then simmer gently for 40 minutes. Strain
the oil through muslin (cheesecloth), pressing to extract all the oil from the petals. Stir in the liquid storax and tincture
of benzoin to fix the fragrance, pour into bottles, seal, label and store in a dry, dark place.

For a relaxing and fragrant bath oil, mix one part home-made floral or herbal oil (p.16) with three parts almond oil
for an oil which will float on the water, or with Turkey red dispersing oil. Pour the oil into bottles, seal, label and store.
These bath oils make excellent gifts. Only a teaspoonful is needed in the bath.

To counteract the drying nature of soap, add a cupful of herbal vinegar (p.16) to your bath water.

HERBAL POWDERS

Make small quantities of fragrant powders to brush lightly on the skin after a bath–all you need to do is grind the
following ingredients together until they are very fine. Mix 30 g/1 oz/ 1⁄4 cup each of dried rose petals, lavender flowers
and ground orris root with 60 g/2 oz/ 1⁄4 cup of cornflour (cornstarch).

NEXT PAGE: Cosmetics fragrant oils and soap using herbal recipes

 # HERB SHAMPOO

Use camomile for fair hair, rosemary or sage leaves
or lavender flowers for dark hair and marigold petals
for red hair. Eggs add protein to the shampoo and
make it richer; for greasy hair, use egg whites only.

1.5 litres/2 ³4 pints/7 cups	*boiling water*
250ml/8 fl oz/1 cup	*herbs or petals*
90 ml/3 fl oz/5 tablespoons	*grated castile soap*
2	*eggs (optional)*

Pour the water over the herbs or petals, stir well, cover and leave to infuse for 2 hours. Strain into a saucepan, pressing all the moisture from the herbs. Stir in the soap and whisk the mixture over a low heat until the soap has dissolved. Leave to cool slightly then whisk in the eggs, if using, pour into bottles and label. Shake the bottle well before using and rinse thoroughly after use.

CONDITIONERS & RINSES

The herbs suggested for shampoos for different hair colours can be used in conditioners and rinses as well, or you can try peppermint or nettle leaves, elder or yarrow flowers or fennel seeds. As a scalp conditioner, mix equal quantities of almond oil and herb oil (p.16) and warm them slightly. Rub the oil into the scalp, wrap a warm towel around your head and leave for 15 minutes before shampooing and rinsing. For a richer conditioner, mix a teaspoon of fragrant oil (p.56) and an egg into 4 tablespoons of plain yoghurt and apply in the same way.

Add a few spoonfuls of herbal vinegar (p.16) to the final rinsing water for healthy, shining hair, or make specific herbal hair rinses. For a lemon hair rinse for greasy hair, mix the grated rind of 2 lemons, 2 tablespoons of chopped lemon balm leaves and 600 ml/1 pint/2½ cups of water in a saucepan, bring to the boil, then simmer for 15 minutes. Remove from the heat and leave to infuse for 2 hours. Strain well then stir in the juice of 2 lemons, pour into bottles, seal and label.

Rosemary hair rinse is said to stimulate the scalp and help to prevent dandruff. Place 60 g/2 oz/1½ cup of rosemary sprigs and 1 litre/1¾ cups/4¼ cups of water in a saucepan, bring to the boil and boil for 15 minutes. Strain, stir in 90 ml/3 fl oz/5 tablespoons of white wine vinegar and 1 tablespoon of lemon juice and store in an airtight jar.

OPPOSITE: Herbal skin lotions, Hair conditioners and rinses using herbal recipes

 # FRAGRANT OILS

Natural oils which encapsulate the fragrance of the
flower or herb form the essence of many cosmetics.

Concentrated herbal oils must be purchased from a herbalist or chemist as there is great skill in preparing such items. However, the following instructions will enable you to create light floral oils with scented flower petals. Use a measuring jug to weigh the petals.

300 ml/ 1⁄2 pint/11⁄4 cups	almond oil
2.25 litres/4 pints/21⁄2 quarts	flower petals
1 teaspoon	liquid storax
1 teaspoon	tincture of benzoin

Warm the oil in the top of a double saucepan over simmering water. Add 450 ml/ 3⁄4 pint/2 cups of petals, stir, cover and leave over a low heat for 2 hours, checking regularly to ensure that the pan does not boil dry. Strain and reserve the flowers. Add another 450 ml/ 3⁄4 pint/2 cups of flowers to the oil and repeat the process until all the flowers have been used.

Pour the oil and all the flowers into a large pan, bring to the boil slowly then simmer gently for 40 minutes. Strain the oil through muslin (cheesecloth), pressing to extract all the oil from the petals. Stir in the liquid storax and tincture of benzoin to fix the fragrance, pour into bottles, seal, label and store in a dry, dark place.

For a relaxing and fragrant bath oil, mix one part home-made floral or herbal oil (p.16) with three parts almond oil for an oil which will float on the water, or with Turkey red dispersing oil. Pour the oil into bottles, seal, label and store. These bath oils make excellent gifts. Only a teaspoonful is needed in the bath.

To counteract the drying nature of soap, add a cupful of herbal vinegar (p.16) to your bath water.

 ## HERBAL SKIN LOTIONS

Herbal lotions can be used for washing, added to
bath water, hair rinses or to scent water for washing
clothes and laundry.

Pour boiling water over 250 ml/8 fl oz/1 cup of fragrant herbs–bergamot, lavender, lemon balm, sage, camomile, marjoram, mint, rosemary, sweet cicely or thyme–so they are just covered, simmer over a low heat for 10 minutes, leave to stand until cool and then strain. Equal quantities of water and wine vinegar with sage and rue leaves and 1 teaspoon of ground ginger, make an unusual toilet water. For an instant herbal bath, place a few herbs in a muslin (cheesecloth) bag with a spoonful of oatmeal to soften the water and hang the bag beneath the hot tap on the bath. Herbal vinegars (p.16) can be added to bath water, washing water, hair rinsing water or water used to wash clothes.

Camomile flowers make a delightful foam bath. Crush 4 tablespoons of dried camomile flowers and mix with 150ml/ 1 4 pint/ 2 3 cup of boiling water and an equal quantity of grated soap. When the mixture has blended, stir in a teaspoon of flower oil to add to the fragrance.

Even ordinary milk can be transformed into a light moisturizing milk by mixing 4 tablespoons of chopped parsley with 300 ml/ 1 2 pint/1 1 4 cups of milk and chilling overnight. The moisturizing milk is then ready for use but must be stored in the refrigerator.

A tablespoon of herbal vinegar added to 150 ml/ 1 4 pint/ 2 3 cup of water or rainwater makes an excellent toner for greasy skin. For normal or dry skin, use 150 ml/ 1 4 pint/ 2 3 cup of rose water, 3 tablespoons of orange flower water and 3 tablespoons of glycerine to make a soothing skin tonic.

Mint has many cosmetic uses, including as a skin toner. Infuse 2 tablespoons of chopped apple mint in 3 tablespoons of white wine vinegar for a week, shaking daily, then strain the vinegar and pour on 300 ml/ 1 2 pint/ 1 1 4 cups of boiling water. Leave to cool, then bottle, seal and label. Mint also makes a refreshing face mask. Simmer 4 tablespoons of chopped mint with 4 tablespoons of water for 5 minutes then remove from the heat and stir in 1 tablespoon of clear honey, 3 tablespoons of milk and 2 tablespoons of fine oatmeal. Leave to cool then apply to the face and leave for at least 15 minutes before rinsing off with lukewarm water.

 # HERBAL CRAFTS

Herbs are not only valuable in the kitchen, in cosmetics and medicines, they are also very beautiful and can be used, both fresh and dried, to decorate and scent your home or as charming gifts.

Fresh Herb Arrangements

Herbs can be made into decorative and fragrant arrangements either alone or with other garden flowers. Rosemary, sage, borage, feverfew, marjoram, lemon balm, thyme, chives, mint, camomile and parsley are all attractive either in leaf or in flower, while seed heads of fennel, caraway or dill add contrast and interest.

A limited colour range often works best; include variety of texture as well as of leaf shape. Most containers can be used but country-style pottery looks particularly attractive, especially as informal arrangements suit herbs best. Evergreen herbs, such as sage and rosemary, make excellent foliage backgrounds for brighter flowers, especially in winter when options for fresh arrangements are limited. Use dry florist's foam (styrofoam) held in place with a spike or tape, to help you to shape your arrangement.

Posies of fresh herbs make delightful gifts or table decorations. Tie a few herb sprigs into a posy, slit a small doily to the centre and wrap it around the back of the posy to resemble a lace frill. Finish with a pretty ribbon. A handful of posies in a basket makes a pretty and fragrant table-centre decoration.

Dried Herb Arrangements

Herbs make excellent additions to your dried flower arrangements, whether you use seed heads, flower stems, leaves or grasses. Follow the same design principles as you would when creating a fresh arrangement. For dried arrangements, your choice of containers is unlimited as they do not need to be watertight and baskets really come into their own. If the materials are fragile, wire the stems or wire bunches of stems together.

Dried herbal wreaths can be made using a florist's foam (styrofoam) ring, available from good florists, or you can bind thick twine or straw round a circle of wire. Use dense leaves, such as bay, to form a dark background then gradually build up a pattern of sprigs of lavender, rosemary, sage and other herbs. You can vary this idea by making dried arrangements on spheres of dry florist's foam (styrofoam).

OPPOSITE: Fresh and dried herb arrangements

Keep pot-pourri in bowls topped with a dried flower
buds, or in pretty glass jars with a lace covering, in
little sachets of lace or special pot-pourri containers.

The simplest way to make pot-pourri is to dry fragrant leaves and petals until they are crisp, blend them with fixatives
to absorb and preserve the scent and seal them in an airtight container for about four weeks to mature, shaking the
mixture occasionally. A few drops of commercial pot-pourri oil adds that final touch and this can also be used to liven
up pot-pourri as the fragrance fades.

For colour, use herbs such as roses and marigolds with garden flowers such as pansies, lily of the valley, orange
blossom, hyacinth or cornflowers. Many herb leaves and flowers provide fragrance: bergamot, basil, bay, thyme,
rosemary, lemon balm, camomile or lavender with garden flowers such as jasmine, mimosa, honeysuckle, carnation
or pinks. A little spice, either cardamom, cinnamon, cloves, ginger, mace, or citrus rind, adds sharpness and interest.

As a rough guide, mix about 900 ml/1½ pints/3¾ cups of flower petals and herb leaves with 2 tablespoons of
spices and 4 tablespoons of fixative. There are many fixatives you can use but ground orris root is simple and effective.
This mixture will need two or three drops of essential oil. Here are some suggestions for pot-pourri recipes:

RECIPE 1	250 ml/8 fl oz/1 cup each	lemon verbena and lemon balm leaves
	250 ml/8 fl oz/1 cup each	forsythia, marigold and camomile flowers
		A few thin strips of lemon rind
	60 g/2 oz/¼ cup	ground orris root
		A few drops of lemon verbena oil

RECIPE 2	250 ml/8 fl oz/1 cup each	thyme, rosemary and mint leaves
	450 ml/¾ pint/2 cups	lavender flowers
	2 tablespoons	tansy leaves
	2 tablespoons	ground cloves
	60 g/2 oz/¼ cup	ground orris root
		A few drops of lavender oil

RECIPE 3	250 ml/8 fl oz/1 cup	lavender flowers
	2 tablespoons each	thyme and mint leaves
	1 tablespoon each	ground cloves and ground caraway seeds

OPPOSITE: A selection of attractive gifts using herbs

 ## LAVENDER BOTTLES

Traditionally used to scent linen drawers and keep away moths, lavender bottles require long-stemmed lavender flowers, picked just as they come into flower. Tie together a bunch of about 20 stalks just below the flower heads, then bend the stalks up and over the flower heads and tie again above the flowers so that they are enclosed in the stalks. Trim the ends. Weave a fine ribbon in and out of the stalks to enclose the flower heads.

SCENTED SACHETS

Sachets made of cotton lawn, tied at the top and decorated with a ribbon bow, make lovely gifts or are also nice to keep for yourself! Use 250 ml/8 fl oz/1 cup each of dried lavender flowers and dried rosemary and mix with 250 ml/8 fl oz/ 1 cup of ground orris root and a few drops of oil of roses, or with a few tablespoons of crushed cloves and a tablespoon of powdered dried orange rind.

PRESSED HERB CRAFTS

Pressed herbs (p.14) can be used to make bookmarks, greetings cards and pictures or even to decorate jars for gifts of home-made herbal cosmetics or preserves. Collect together all your materials before you start: a soft paintbrush, rubber-based glue, the pressed petals and leaves and the items you wish to decorate.

Sketch your design roughly then practise positioning the herbs, moving them with a paint brush until you have a pleasing arrangement. Your designs should be simple until you have gained a little experience and confidence; try reproducing a simple flower, bouquet or arrangement.

When you are happy with the design, lift the pieces and apply some glue with a cocktail stick (toothpick). If there are several layers to the design, let one layer dry before adding the next. Cover flat designs with a sheet of glass or board and weigh down with books overnight so that the herbs dry flat. Cover designs on glass or jars with adhesive film or glass, or paint with lacquer to protect them. Pressed flower pictures should be kept out of direct sunlight so that they do not fade.

 # INDEX